Wicca And Spells Made Simple

Welcome to the wonderful world of Wicca and Mag

This book is specially designed to make the path of simple, affordable, easy to access and fun.

As you may know, there are 1000s of books out there about Magic, Wicca and witchcraft. As good as these books are, they can sometimes be full of spells and ingredients that make it almost impossible or too expensive to practise.

Some of the books can also bombard your mind with complicated philosophy which can easily baffle or confuse even the most experienced of witches.

It is my belief that everyone should be able to enjoy and practise Wicca and magic no matter what level of experience you have and that is why with a little help from others we have come up with this simple guide to help you on your wonderful path of a new way forward.

In this book there are also note pages for you to record your own experiences, thoughts and wishes, this is the start of what we call 'The Book of Shadows'. In your book you record and keep everything that you have and need for your magical journey.

This will be discussed in the next few chapters.

So, sit down, open up and let your journey begin….

Chapter 1: The Wiccan Way of Life

Chapter 2: The Wiccan Rede

Chapter 3: What is Wicca used or?

Chapter 4: Wiccan Holidays

Chapter 5: Tools you may need

Chapter 6: The Four Elements

Chapter 7: Setting up your Altar

Chapter 8: Magic as a tool

Chapter 9: How to use a Crystal Ball

Chapter 10: Smudging

Chapter 11: Circle Casting and the Four Elements

Chapter 12: Broomsticks

Chapter 13: Divination

Chapter 14: Spells, Tools and Ingredients needed for Spells

Chapter 15: Thought forms

Chapter 16: Hoodoo Dolls

Chapter 17: Books of Shadows

Chapter 18: Mojo Bags

Chapter 19: Wiccan Ways to use Herbs

Chapter 20: Candle Magic

Chapter 21: Crystals

Chapter 22: Aromatherapy Oils

Chapter 23: Spell Directory

Conclusion

Chapter 1: The Wiccan Way of Life

Wicca promotes a very peaceful, harmonious and balanced way of life, which encourages oneness with the divine and all that exists. Wicca is a practice that brings you a deep appreciation for the energy of the Earth and the elements and the energy of the divine.

Wicca is a divine path and much of the practice is devoted to Mother Nature and the respect for all Gods and Goddesses of Earth.

In Wicca, your intention and your belief set the stage, no matter what kind of ritual you are using. It does not have to be complicated; the simpler the ritual, the more effective it will become.

If you don't have a positive intention and the will to succeed, it wouldn't matter if the spell you were using were 1000 years old or brand new, as the person practising the ritual or spell determines its success.

The important thing to remember for many of us, (and this is really good news) is that the power lies in you. If you try a ritual out for size and it doesn't seem like the right one for you, feel free to choose another or even create your own! In order for the practice to be effective, the ritual must speak to you.

Wicca is not evil and the practice is not about devil worship; never believe what Hollywood says! Films have often portrayed Wicca as negative! This is far from the truth.

The Wiccan religion can be controversial. Christians seem to believe Wiccans are brainwashed devil-worshipers who are part of a cult. Nothing could be further from the truth.

There have been many arguments when it comes to defining the Wiccan religion and it has been much debated over the years. In many ways, Wiccan is not that different from Christianity, or any other religious practice; look at the similarities of some of our celebrations, which we will cover later on.

Even, within Christianity, the core principles are not always clear. Though the idea of Christianity is simple enough, it's not that easy to interpret what it really means to be Christian. As a matter of fact, one can be a Christian and Wiccan at the same time, even though that might seem strange to some; remember it is what comes from your heart that is important.

Wiccans practise witchcraft as part of their particular religion, though you don't actually need to be Wiccan in order to cast spells or do rituals, which may be a little confusing.

What it is, is a beautiful, sacred practice where you connect with the divine. It supports you and protects you and helps you find peace and well-being.

Wicca was originally designed to be taught within a coven; however, this is no longer the case. However, I can't stress enough that practicing in a group can help bring you closer to others and helps you to develop a support network.

As time has passed, there have been many books and publications on Wicca so a coven is no longer necessary. However, as I said at the beginning of this book, these can sometimes make the practice confusing and expensive.

Wicca's origins are based more on pagan beliefs and practices, or on practices where one pursues one's own vision of the Divine as a direct and personal experience. Most of these beliefs came about before the spread of Christianity.

Many Wiccans adopt aspects from Pagan practices to enhance their Wiccan practice. This is in line with Wiccan beliefs which identify that we must do what we feel most comfortable with and are all capable of achieving.

I feel that the most important aspect of Wicca is that you "First do no harm". This is the mantra of "what you put out there comes back on you three times three"; beware of doing negative spells.

Now this does not mean that you have to be weak and let others walk all over you. There are ways around this as we shall learn later.

The Law of Three times Three

Always remember that everything you put out comes back on you three fold. Never use magic to do harm to others as this will come back on you three times.

Chapter 2: The Wiccan Rede

Wicca is an Earth religion. It is an accepting, open-minded faith that celebrates diversity and a faith that considers us all children of the same Mother.

Wicca does not discriminate against gender, race, age, sexual orientation, ethnic heritage or family background. This makes Wicca a very modern practice for a lot of people from all works of life.

Wicca has no central organisation, no governing body, no supreme leader and no high priestess who acts as a Goddess.

The Wiccan temple might be comprised of a garden, a forest, a beach or even a bookstore. Wicca is a faith that accepts everyone, and a faith that encourages everyone to take their own spiritual path. This is great because there is no pressure on you and you can do as much or as little as you like.

Wicca can be looked at as an organic religion, or one that is evolving and emerging as a worldwide faith.

Wicca is a way of life and a belief system. The way we interact with the world around us, reflects our personal commitment to the Wiccan principles.

Wicca's highest priorities are personal integrity and respect for Mother Nature, which is a beautiful thing.

The Wiccan faith has two distinct pillars - The Great Goddess and the poem called "The Wiccan Rede."

The first step to becoming a witch is to find your own unique way to the Goddess.

The second is to establish an ethical system to use the gift of magic. This is called "The Wiccan Rede".

"The Wiccan Rede."

Bide within the Law you must, in perfect Love and perfect Trust.
Live you must and let to live, fairly take and fairly give.

For tread the Circle thrice about to keep unwelcome spirits out.
To bind the spell well every time, let the spell be said in rhyme.

Light of eye and soft of touch, speak you little, listen much.
Honour the Old Ones in deed and name, let love and light be our guides again.

Deosil go by the waxing moon, chanting out the joyful tune.
Widdershins go when the moon doth wane, and the werewolf howls by the dread wolfsbane.

When the Lady's moon is new, kiss the hand to Her times two.
When the moon rides at Her peak then your heart's desire seek.

Heed the North winds mighty gale, lock the door and trim the sail.
When the Wind blows from the East, expect the new and set the feast.

When the wind comes from the South, love will kiss you on the mouth.
When the wind whispers from the West, all hearts will find peace and rest.

Nine woods in the Cauldron go, burn them fast and burn them slow.
Birch in the fire goes to represent what the Lady knows.

Oak in the forest towers with might, in the fire it brings the God's insight.
Rowan is a tree of power causing life and magic to flower.

Willows at the waterside stand ready to help us to the Summerland.
Hawthorn is burned to purify and to draw faerie to your eye.

Hazel-the tree of wisdom and learning adds its strength to the bright fire burning.
White are the flowers of Apple tree that brings us fruits of fertility.

Grapes grow upon the vine giving us both joy and wine.
Fir does mark the evergreen to represent immortality seen.

Elder is the Lady's tree burn it not or cursed you'll be.
Four times the Major Sabbats mark in the light and in the dark.

As the old year starts to wane the new begins, it's now Samhain.
When the time for Imbolc shows, watch for flowers through the snows.

When the wheel begins to turn, soon the Beltane fires will burn.
As the wheel turns to Lamas, night power is brought to magic rite.

Four times the Minor Sabbats fall use the Sun to mark them all.
When the wheel has turned to Yule, light the log the Horned One rules.

In the spring, when night equals daytime for Ostara to come our way.
When the Sun has reached its height, time for Oak and Holly to fight.

Harvesting comes to one and all when the Autumn Equinox does fall.
Heed the flower, bush, and tree by the Lady blessed you'll be.

Where the rippling waters go cast a stone, the truth you'll know.
When you have and hold a need, harken not to others greed.

With a fool no season spend or be counted as his friend.
Merry Meet and Merry Part bright the cheeks and warm the heart.

Mind the Three-fold Laws you should three times bad and three times good.
When misfortune is enow wear the star upon your brow.

Be true in love this you must do unless your love is false to you.

These Eight words the Rede fulfil:
"An Ye Harm None, Do What Ye Will"

You can shorten this version of 'The Wiccan Rede' if you wish or need to do so. To support you, shortened versions can readily be found on the internet.

You can use the space below for personal thoughts and reflections on what you have read.

Chapter 3: What is Wicca used for?

You can use Wicca for many things. It is up to you where you want to take your path; here is a list of things you may want to use your magic to manifest:

- Matters of love.
- Increase prosperity and abundance.
- Gain more success.
- Enhance personal power.
- Protection and security.
- Boost health.
- Boost good luck.

With Wicca, love, money, beauty, and success are all within your reach.

Rituals, oils, and herbs are all used in conjunction with your good faith and intentions. However, it is important to keep in mind that you also have to take some action in order to see success; things won't just fall into your lap!

There are four-steps to follow in order for your spells and magic to work. These are:

1. Constructive will
2. Creative imagination (also known as the 'thought form')
3. Faith
4. Secrecy

This four-step process is used in all rituals.

Your **constructive will** gives focus to your energy.

This harnessing of energy is required to help you bring your desires to life. This is known as a '**thought form**'. We will learn more about this later.

This thought form is nurtured by your **faith** and fed with a regular dose of love and enthusiasm.

This thought form is protected by your **secrecy** until it manifests.

This formula uses the four points on the base of the Witch's Pyramid

The Witch's Pyramid, known as the four Pillars of the Witches' Temple, forms the foundation for all magic work. It represents a mindset necessary to create magic and the qualities all witches should embrace.

The four statements that represent the Witch's Pyramid are:
- To know
- To will
- To dare
- To keep silent

Each of these is required in order to perform magic.

The Witch's Pyramid is made up of the four main elements that coincide with the four cardinal directions (North, East, South, West) and the four elements of earth, fire air and water.

To Know – Corresponds to Air
'To know' refers to the knowledge and understanding of the work at hand. This means understanding all aspects of the work from rituals, casting spells,

candle magic, crystals, spirit connection, ceremony, divination etc. The more the tools are understood, the more powerful and effective they are.

A witch must manage and work with the energies that are invoked, and this is not something to be taken lightly.

Most practitioners already have an innate knowing and understanding beyond the five senses, which is most likely what draws them to the craft in the first place.

To Will – Corresponds to Fire
'To will' is the way in which you conduct your life. Your belief and commitment to any spell or ritual are critically important. Your will allows you to raise, manipulate, manage, and maintain both focus and attention.

To will has much to do with your conviction and energy to manifest magic. A practitioner must know how to summon and direct energy and work with their internal drive, will, want, and focus, which all leads to manifestation (the realisation of the magic).

In order to create magic, a witch has to believe unequivocally in the magic they are creating. Anyone hoping to manifest needs to understand that will is an integral part of magic.

To Dare – Corresponds to Water
A Wiccan must dare to do magic without fear and must be daring to experiment, push forward and try new things.

A practitioner must dare to go beyond those physical limitations and surrender to the universal energies, as they travel to astral realms.

Daring to be part of the cosmic order and letting the energies flow is an important part of the craft.

Transcending those inner fears and perceived barriers and meeting with deities and spirits is also part of the fun, but it must be taken seriously. Facing whatever needs to be faced and overcoming it helps a witch hone their craft.

When a witch wields magic, their personal emotions play a key part and a witch must always be ready to meet a challenge.

To Keep Silent – Corresponds with Earth
When you allow yourself to be silent, you can hear the message more easily. Some things are better off being quietly understood and don't necessarily need to be shared.

Just because you know, this doesn't mean that others should know also. Understanding that your inner-silence and carefully grounding yourself and centring are all key in magical work and are essential to maintaining a clear intent.

When invoking the gods and goddesses, a still and clear channel is necessary for an effective and powerful connection.

When invoking and receiving messages, there must be silence to hear the channelled wisdom.

Now have a rest and have a brew. Let your mind absorb what you have read.

The next few pages are a little exercise for you. You can write down the reasons why you want to follow the wiccan way and what you hope to achieve.

Why have I chosen the Wiccan way and what I hope to achieve.

"Instead of cursing the darkness, light a candle"

Chapter 4: Wiccan Holidays

Holidays and Days of Power

Every religion has its own days of celebration, reverence and power and Wicca is no different. The holidays that Wiccans celebrate are known as Sabbats, or the Eight High Holy Days. The sun, as a representation of the God, is revered during each Sabbat.

The Eight Major Sabbats

As Wiccans we celebrate eight Sabbats or sacred days every year, and those dates usually correspond to a new phase of life, a seasonal changes or historical harvest times. You may think that there are a lot of similarities with major Christian holidays. This is true. Early Christians combined pagan holidays with their own to encourage pagans to convert to Christianity.

> **Yule** – December 21 (Winter solstice)
> **Candlemas/imbolc** – February 2 (Groundhog Day)
> **Ostara** – March 21 (Spring Equinox)
> **Beltane** – May 1 (Previously celebrated on May 5 or Mayday)
> **Midsummer** – June 21 (Summer Solstice)
> **Lammas** – August 1 (Harvest Eve)
> **Mabon** – September 21 (Autumn Equinox)
> **Samhain** – October 31 (All Hallows' Eve or Halloween)

These phases typically celebrate the God, though many practitioners incorporate an aspect of the Goddess in some form as well.

They are primarily Sun festivals and, unlike Esbats, the rituals are often done when the sun is at its highest.

Sabbats are usually large gatherings where entire families come together to celebrate with food and drink in addition to the religious rites.

Here is a brief explanation as to what each one means.

SAMHAIN

Samhain is probably the most recognisable of all the Wiccan Sabbats. In some cultures, it signifies Halloween or All Hallows' Eve.
The date falls on October 31st and signifies the end of one cycle of the year.

The main symbolism behind this holiday is death and honouring those loved ones who have passed on. There is a lot of folklore which identifies that the veil between worlds is at its thinnest at this time and witches can take advantage of this opportunity to communicate with their family and friends who have passed on.

YULE

Yule is generally thought to coincide with the Christian holiday of Christmas; however, this may not be entirely accurate.

Yule actually falls on the day of the Winter Solstice, which generally falls around December 21st. The exact date of the Winter Solstice depends on the position of the moon each year.

The holiday signifies rebirth; the days grow longer and the sun starts making its comeback.

This holiday represents the Goddess giving birth to the God, the child of promise who is reborn with the retuning sun.

Yule is a joyous celebration of peace, love and positive energy for friends and family. Witches incorporate ancient pagan traditions into their festivities.

These traditions include Yule logs, gift giving, wassail cups, mistletoe charms, and bringing evergreens into the home or decorating a tree.

CANDLEMAS

Candlemas is also known by the name Imbolc. This holiday represents the quickening of the year. This is time when winter blossom appears on the bare trees and green life starts to stir under the frozen earth.

The infant sun or the god also grows in size and strength. Imbolc is a fire festival, a festival of lights, and a festival sacred to the Irish goddess Brighid.

Witches light candles to illuminate the winter darkness and start spring-cleaning.

The specific date that this day falls on varies from tradition, but it can be anywhere from Jan 31st – Feb 2nd. This holiday also signifies Groundhog Day in some cultures.

The festivities for Candlemas all centre on clearing out the old and making way for the new.

The maiden aspect of the Goddess is also honoured at this time, as are any Gods and Goddesses that relate to love and fertility. This holiday is considered and especially good time for a new marriage or relationship.

OSTARA

Also called Eastar, this holiday signifies the Spring Equinox on or near the 21st March. This is the second of the three fertility festivals. This is a time when spring is coming in full force or planting for the year's crops is also well underway. The new spring growth is now apparent and the Gods are petitioned for luck with the crops and the home.

Two of the traditional symbols for this holiday are the egg and the rabbit. Witches follow the old tradition of dyeing and painting hard boiled eggs and balancing eggs on their ends to symbolise equilibrium.

The egg is a symbol of new life and new growth, and it is incorporated into many ritual workings and festivities. The rabbit is known for its prolific mating habits and is a symbol of growth and abundance. Both the egg and the rabbit symbolise change.

BELTANE

This holiday occurs around the festival known as Mayday. It is the last of the fertility festivals for the year and with it comes unabashed sexual activity, according to many of the traditions.

The May pole is a symbol of this holiday and is found throughout many traditions. It is a tall pole set in the ground, symbolising the Sun God uniting with Earth. The May pole is decorated with long ribbons and fresh flowers, and, of course, maidens traditionally dance around the pole. The May pole is commonly recognised as a phallic symbol.

Generally, this holiday celebrates and revels in the return of the sun.

MIDSUMMER

This Holy Day celebrates the God, (represented by the sun in all of his glory), and is also known as the Summer Solstice (linked to the longest day of the year). Midsummer is neither a fertility festival nor a harvest festival. On this day, rites often centre on:
- protection for the home and family for the coming year,
- rites of divination,
- celebrating the abundance of the Oak King in his prime of life.

At Midsummer, the Earth is in full bloom and the mother is pregnant. The King of Summer is also at the peak of his powers.

For those who work with faerie energy in their rites, Midsummer is an ideal time to commune with fairies. It is common tradition for witches to go out in the twilight and look for faeries.

LAMMAS

Another name for this holiday is Lughnassadh. Lammas occurs on August 1st and it is the first of the three harvest sabbats celebrated by witches. The days grow shorter, and the crops are ready to be harvested. Preparations also begin for the coming winter.

As this is the time of year when we first begin to reap bounties of harvest, it is often a holiday accompanied with feasting and celebration.

Decorations and dolls are often made from dried ears of corn and used in rituals and to decorate the home.

MABON

Mabon is the primary harvest festival, known as Autumn Equinox. On this day, witches pay homage to retreating daylight whilst preparing for the coming winter. This holiday symbolises the God in his old age, readying for his impending death and rebirth.

Though this holiday is a little lower key than others, it is also a time where Wiccans are sure to give thanks for what they have received throughout the past year.

It is a popular time of year for witches and pagans to give back to their communities and generally share their bountiful harvests.

THE ESBAT

The Esbat is a ceremony that coincides with the cycles of the moon.

The Esbat is a monthly occurrence that typically coincides with the full moon. The full moon is often a popular time for Wiccans, as they gather to perform magical spells and rituals. The moon is significant because Wiccans often work with the moon in its waxing or waning phase.

When the moon is waxing (or becoming fuller), it is a good time to perform rites that are meant to draw things to you. The waxing moon also signifies positive influences.

When the moon is waning (or diminishing), it is a good time for banishing influences that are no longer wanted. The waning moon is also a good time for getting rid of negativity.

When the moon is full, the magical workings are at their peak, so it is a good time for nearly any rite. The new moon, or dark moon, occurs when the moon is not visible. The new moon is a good time to perform rituals for protection.

No matter what day the Esbat is performed, it is done in the evening or at night since these rites are meant to be working with the Goddess, who is represented by the moon.

Performing the Esbats

Performing the Esbat is fairly simple.

The witches will gather at a designated ritualistic space and cast a simple circle. The next step involves raising the magical and psychic powers and then directing that power towards the desired goal.

If done in a group, this is a good time for communing with a deity and connecting. The Wiccan Rede may also be recited before the work at hand begins. After the work is complete, the ritual circle is then opened, and any leftover food or wine is offered up to nature.

Wiccans often change the layout of their altar to match the season being celebrated. A Wiccan is free to choose the items they have on their altar as well as how these are placed on the altar. An altar can be as simple of complex as each Wiccan desires.

Remember that the earth will provide many items we can use. It is important to remember that we must respect Mother Nature when gathering items for the altar. We should be mindful not to create damage and to ensure future provision is not disturbed. It is also important to thank Mother Nature for her provisions.

The Goddess stares at the Horned God "All is good with the world"

Chapter 5: Tools you may need

Tools

Tools are the implements used to work magic. The best approach to take is a minimalist approach, adding to your own collection as time goes on. If you try and collect all of the tools before doing any work, you may never get around to doing any actual work!

It is not necessary to acquire everything on the list, so you can use your best judgment. Tools are used along with an altar, which can also be very simple. Use whatever tools and materials feel right for you, and don't get too caught up in trying to make everything perfect.

You can start by making or acquiring tools as you need them. You may even find that tools magically appear when you need them, which can be a lot of fun.

Conflicting superstitions about tools:

- They have to be formally consecrated before use.
- Tools should only be used inside of a circle.
- Using tools in the kitchen actually consecrates the food they are used to prepare.
- Tools must be made by you or received as gifts.
- If you haggle over a tool, it is bad luck.
- You should never allow anyone else to handle your tools.
- The finest tools are those you make yourself, from natural materials.
- Any sword, knife or dagger that has ever drawn blood must be purified before consecration.
- Athames and swords, should be symbolic, not actual weapons.

The best rule of thumb once again is to use your intuition and your best judgement. In other words, you may choose to accept or reject these beliefs as seems right to you. Some practitioners never consecrated their tools whilst others make it a standard part of their practice.
Some practitioners even believe that the use of magic is self-consecrating while others disagree.

It is a good idea to keep your tools to yourself because other people's energy may cause a disturbance.

Consecration
Consecration is a short ceremony that is used to dedicate an object for sacred use. The good news is you can use any sacred ceremony that feels right to you.

A simple ceremony may go something like this:
- Lay your tool or tools on your altar.
- Cast a circle and call in the four corners.
- Sprinkle the tool with salt water from the altar.
- Recite a short phase like "I bring this tool within this circle for magical transformation". You could also say "knife, you are brought into this sacred circle to be forever my athame".
- Handle the object with care, immersing it in your vibration, placing it on an altar.
- Close the sacred circle.

(Casting a circle and calling the four corners will be explained later)

This simple ceremony can be used to turn a branch into a wand, a glass into a chalice, or a pot into a cauldron.

List of Tools

Athame

An athame is a ceremonial knife that corresponds to the element of fire in some traditions, air in others.

The athame is used for:
- Mixing salt and water, or potions.
- Inscribing the circle.
- Charging, consecrating, or empowering amulets, talismans, or poppets.
- Drawing lines.
- Discrimination and setting limits.
- Making choices and carrying them out.

Bells

Bells or gongs are sometimes used as part of a ritual as well. A bell can be rung to banish spirits, entities, negative energy or anything else. It can also signify the beginning or ending of a ritual. A bell can also be used to summon good spirits.

Bowls

Bowls are used to hold water, salt and earth. An altar typically has two bowls, one for salt water and one for earth. You may use any bowls that feel special to you.

Broomstick

Broomsticks are mainly symbolic and can be used for cleansings, sweeping away evil spirits or negative influences, expelling evil spirits and purification.

Cauldron
A cauldron signifies the womb of the Goddess. Its energy is female and its element is water.

A cauldron is used for:
- Brewing herbs and potions.
- Renewal.
- Reflecting the moon.
- Jumping over for fertility.
- Safely burning things.

Crystals
Quartz crystals are very popular today. The sphere is an ancient magical tool and the crystal has long been used for contemplative divination. You can gaze into the crystal until you feel creative insight coming on, or you can simply use crystals or stones in your magical rituals.

In Wiccan ritual, crystals are sometimes placed on the altar to represent the Goddess.

Incense
Incense is used for fumigating and smudging, purifying, raising power, achieving trance states, banishing evil spirits, and encouraging and welcoming good spirits.

Pentacle / Pentagram
The pentacle (also called pentagram) is usually a flat piece of brass, gold, silver, wood, wax or clay, inscribed with certain symbols. The most common one is the five-pointed star that is often linked to magical rituals.

The pentacle represents the element earth and is often used as an instrument for protection. You can place amulets, crystals, charms or other objects upon on them or hang the pentacle over a door or window to protect the dwelling.

Sword

A sword is used just like an athame, but it is much more formal. A sword could be an actual weapon or simply a ceremonial object.

You could use your sword for:
- Invoking the Lords of the Watchtowers
- Ruling the circle
- Making salutations

Wand

A wand is used in a similar way to a sword or an athame. Wands were traditionally cut from one-year old trees, in a single stroke at sunrise or on a Wednesday. Wands can be made of wood or metal.

If you choose to cut your wand from a tree, ask permission first and then make sure to leave it a gift or offering. Choosing a branch from a fallen tree or piece of driftwood might be preferable.
Wands are used for:

Casting circles, channelling energy, manifestation and inviting and controlling entities.

Personally, I believe that the wand is the most important tool for any Wiccan.

Book of Shadows

This is a book in which you record all your magical dealings, thoughts, spells and so on. There are further details about the Book of Shadows later in this book.

Chapter 6: The Four Elements

In magic and before carrying out any ritual we need to use the four elements. These are 'Earth', 'Air', 'Fire' and 'Water'. These make up each corner of the pentagram with Spirit bringing in the 5th point.

The elements of earth, air, fire and water are the foundations of magic and sacred to the Hindu Goddess Shakti, who embodies the concept of energy. All rituals should contain one of these four elements whenever a spell is cast.

They are usually represented by:

Earth = Salt
Air = Incense
Fire = Candles
Water = Water

When doing rituals, you may feel an affinity towards certain elements over others and this will most likely influence your style of practising magic.

The charts below offer a list of the four elements and their related items.

Earth

Used For - Money spells, rock magic, fertility

Planet - Earth, Saturn and Venus

Time – Midnight

Season – Winter

Quality - Emotional, melancholic, feminine

Direction – North

Jewel - Salt, rock salt, agate, bloodstone, smoky quartz, carnelian, tiger's eye, emerald

Tool – Pentacle

Zodiac - Taurus (fixed earth), Virgo (mutable earth), Capricorn (cardinal earth)

Colour - Black, brown, green and white

Incense - Benzoin, fumitory (earth smoke), Storax

Symbol - Grain, globe, orb, stones, acorns, cornucopia, soil, pottery, sand

Plant - Adonis, amaranth, barley, comfrey, grain, hops, ivy, maize, liquorice, millet, oak, oats, rice, root vegetables, rye, wheat

Animal - Cattle, bison, stag, earth-dwelling snakes, mole, dragon (earth energy), sphinx

Rules - Life, birth, growth, nature, money, food, prosperity, silence, wisdom, agriculture, creativity, canyons, caverns, chasms, rocks, caves, metals, agriculture, crystals, matter, stability, strength, trees, bones, mountains, the body, physical reality, standing stones, the sense of touch, the first astral plane, the ability of life to sustain itself

Invocations - Gnomes, grain and mountain god/goddesses, the sidh, sphinxes

Air

Used For - Psychic work

Planet – Jupiter

Time – Dawn

Season – Spring

Quality - Contemplative, Sanguine, masculine

Direction – East

Jewel – Topaz

Tool - Athame, sword, censer

Zodiac - Gemini (mutable air) Libra (cardinal air) Aquarius (fixed air)

Colour - Pastels, white, clear, pale blue, yellow

Incense - Frankincense, fumitory, galibanum, myrrh

Symbol - Incense, feathers, balloons, bubbles, kites, windmills, sails, fans

Plant - Anemone (windflower), aspen, bodhi tree, epiphytic plants (birds nest fern), plants and trees that provide incense, pansy, popular, primrose, vervain, violet, wall fern (polypody) yarrow.

Animal - Bird, insect, eagle, hawk, sphinx

Rules - Thoughts, ideas, flight, knowledge, wind, intellect, breath, learning, intuition, towers, aeries, high and windy places, the mind, the abstract, the mental plane, the sense of smell

Invocations - Fairies, the lilitu (wind spirits), sylphs, sprites, undines, wind god/dess

FIRE

Used For - Purification, sex magic, healing (to destroy disease), candle magic, hearth magic

Planet - Sun, Mars, Jupiter

Time - Noon

Season - Summer

Quality - Destructive, choleric, masculine, phallic

Direction - South

Jewel - Fire, opal, pyrite/firestone, amethyst, fire garnet

Tool - Censer, wand

Zodiac - Aries (cardinal fire) Leo (fixed fire) Sagittarius (mutable fire)

Colour - Red, gold, crimson, orange, white

Incense - Copal, frankincense, rose

Symbol - Swastika (fire wheel), candle, crucible, matches

Plant - Alder, almond tree in bloom dittany (burning bush), fire thorn, flame tree, garlic, hibiscus, mustard, nettles, onion, hot peppers, red poppy, rose

Animal - Salamander, lion, snake, fire-breathing dragon, horse (when their hooves strike sparks), serpent

Rules - Energy, activity, motivation, sight, quickening, blood, sap, spirit, purification, heat, flames, bonfires, lust, life, enthusiasm, passion, the hearth, inspiration, transformation, vitality, sexuality, leadership, combustion, healing.

Invocations - Djinn, hearth and smith, God/ Goddesses, salamander

Water

Used For - Healing, love spells, purification, psychic work, fertility, weather magic

Planet - Moon, Neptune, Saturn, Venus

Time - Twilight

Season - Autumn

Quality - Emotional, phlegmatic, feminine

Direction - West

Jewel - Crystal, coral, sea salt, jade, pearl, mother of pearl

Tool - Chalice, cauldrons

Zodiac - Cancer (cardinal water) Scorpio (fixed water) Pisces (mutable water)

Colour - Blue, black, green, clear

Incense - Lotus, myrrh, aromatic rush roots

Symbol - Pitcher, wave, tear, raindrop, snowflake

Plant - Aquatic plants, ferns, fungi, lotus, moss, reeds, rushes, sea-weed, soma, squill, watercress, water lily, willow

Animal - Sea mammals, marine life, crocodile, salamander, sea birds, water dwelling snake

Rules - Emotions, fertility, sensuality, intuition, change, sorrow, compassion, receptivity, wells and lakes, waterfalls and pools, marine life, psychic ability, the feminine, the subconscious, the womb

Invocations - Mer-folk, water sprites

Use the space below to write notes on which element you feel the greatest affinity towards and why.

Chapter 7: Setting up your Altar

Setting up an altar is one of the most important practices in Wicca. An altar is a place of worship and a place for casting spells.

Creating an altar is a very personal practice and these guidelines are not set in stone. An altar can be a formal altar with elaborate furnishings or it can be simple and created by something like a desk or a table. An altar is ideally set up in a private space solely dedicated to the practice.

A typical altar includes:
- Candles
- Magical tools
- Cauldron.
- Athame
- Bell
- Bowls for salt and water
- Statues or other representations of deities.
- Incense or sage.
- Crystals.
- Chalice
- Wand.
- Offerings, such as fruit and flowers.
- Anything you consider beautiful or sacred.

An altar can be personalised, so feel free to use your imagination. In other words, you can put anything you want on an altar, as long as it makes you feel good.

You can pay homage to a particular God or Goddess, decorate your altar for the seasons/ the sabbats or even the full moon, or whatever feels and looks right to you.

An altar is a wonderful thing to have and a convenient place to work magic. However, if you don't have the ability to create a permanent altar, that's fine too. You can simply place your sacred items on a beautiful tray and move it around as needed. The important thing is that you create some kind of dedicated space to do rituals and spells.

If your circumstances prevent you from erecting an altar, it is certainly possible to manage without one. Temporary altars can be put up and taken back down for a ritual or spell.

There are those who keep supplies for an altar in a box and those who keep a permanent altar are dedicated for the purpose, so there are no rules.

Creating a Sacred Space

A 'Sacred Space' is a dedicated space that is set apart for rituals and magic. You can also use a sacred space for meditation, worship or any other sacred practice.

If you are fortunate enough to have a permanent space, like a dedicated room or garden space, that's wonderful but it's certainly not necessary. A sacred space is a space where you can go to light some candles, burn some incense, or simply pray, so you can decide what kind of space best suits your needs.

To create your temporary sacred space, light some candles, burn incense, or play music you consider sacred. You should then mentally define that area thus making it sacred.

Chapter 8: Magic as tool

Magic is real and it is not something to be taken lightly. When you use magic, you are affecting reality and impacting on things around you.

You should never fool around with magic unless you are serious about the practice because whatever you put into the universe comes back to you in some way, shape or form.

Magic is a very valuable tool, but its power is a double edge sword. When it comes down to it, magic disturbs the known universe, so it's important to save it for the big stuff.

Like anything else in life, you get out of it whatever you put into it, so it pays to do the homework ahead of time to be fully prepared. Although magic is powerful, it is not a quick answer to everything.

When considering a ritual:
- Be realistic in your expectations.
- Recognise situations that might be better dealt with by law enforcement, doctors, or other professionals.
- Be reasonable. If someone is spouting blood, apply a tourniquet and call for help before you even think of doing a stop bleeding spell.

Magic is a natural process as opposed to a supernatural one. Magic is manipulation of energy in order to achieve a desired result. Just like a physicist might study quantum and particles, you can study and apply magic.

In other words, you can change a thing merely by concentrating on it. That's really how magic works. Learning to cast spells successfully is just the starting point.

As a Wiccan, your ultimate goal should be to experience life itself as magical and to honour the Goddess in whatever form she takes.

The life stages of the Goddess.

Maiden, Mother and the Crone represents the three life stages of the Goddess.

This picture symbolises the Goddess in her three stages of Maiden, Mother and Crone above the crescent moon.

Use the space below to write personal requests which you may wish to use in your magic.

Chapter 9: How to Use A Crystal Ball

Crystal gazing (also called scrying) is divination of distant or future events based on vision seen in a ball or rock crystal. Scrying became widespread by the 5th century AD and was condemned by the medieval Christian church as work of the devil.

When you learn how to use a crystal ball it is very important to know how to charge it and how to clean it. When you first purchase a crystal ball and after every scrying session you should clean and charge it.

How to cleanse a crystal ball

To cleanse the ball you can rinse it under running water then place it in some salt water for a short period of time.

You can also pass it through the smoke of sage to cleanse it without soaking it in water if you prefer.

If you can run the crystal ball through a running river or the waves of the ocean it can have a more significant cleansing effect on the crystal.

How to charge a crystal ball

- Cast a circle and call in the four corners.
- Hold the crystal ball in the palms of your hand.
- Close your eyes.
- Imagine a white light coming down through your head, into your shoulders, down through your arms, penetrating the ball through your hands.
- Imagine this light filling the ball with your thoughts and intentions.

You may decide to chant the following *"I bless this ball to bring insight and blessings to my magical deeds. Bring to me positive messages and insight that I need to make my life complete. So mote it be"*

Chapter 10: Smudging with Sage

Sage smudging has been carried out by many cultures throughout the centuries. Smudging with sage is an integral part of the witch's cleansing rites. It is a tool, when used properly, which can be used for the following purposes:

- Warding off negative spirits
- Cleansing and blessing a room
- Healing and protection
- Consecrating items for your altar
- Enhancing thought form
- Aiding medication
- Creating a positive environment for your rituals

Preparation

Ensure that you have the right sage (one that you feel the most comfortable with). For example:
- White sage
- Blue sage
- Dragon's blood sage
- Mixed sage

Prepare your room in the following way:
- Remove any pets or other people from the room
- Open all doors and windows (this allows for all negativity to leave the space)
- Ensure that all cupboards and drawers are open

How To Smudge
1. Light the end of a sage bundle with a match (preferred over a lighter). Blow out quickly if it catches on fire.
2. The tips of the leaves should smoulder slowly, releasing thick smoke. Direct this smoke around your body and space with one hand while holding the bundle in the other.
3. Allow the incense to linger on the areas of your body or surroundings you would like to focus on. Using a fan or feather can also help direct the smoke, though this is optional.
4. Allow the ash to collect in a ceramic bowl or shell.
5. Remember to ensure that doors and windows are open throughout the process.

When smudging chant the following constantly: "*Safe be. Cleansed be. Any badness, leave thee*. So mote it be".

If smudging your home or living space, direct sage smoke over all surfaces and spaces in your home or living area. Be thorough.

You can also light and burn sage to improve odour, fragrance, and mood.

Simply waft sage smoke in and around your home. You can place the bundle in a fireproof bowl or burner and allow it to smoke for a while.

What to do after smudging

Make sure your smudge stick is completely extinguished. You can do this by dabbing the lit end into a small bowl of ash or sand.

Check the end closely to make sure there are no more embers burning.

Once it has completely put out, store it in a safe, dry place out of the sun.

Chapter 11: Casting your Circle and Calling of the Four Elements

Before doing any form of magic or spell work you must cast your circle and then call in the four corners or elements.

Before you start you need to cast your protective circle.

Casting a protection circle which is where you hold your wand in the air and turn clock wise and maybe say the following.

"I cast this circle in love, light and protection for all those here and to protect me during my magical work so mote it be".

Everyone in the circle is now safe. You may start your magic.

Remember when you have finished close the circle anti-clockwise and chant *"I close this circle in love, light and peace so mote it be"*.

To call the four elements you raise your hands and say the following:

"I call upon the guardians of North, elements of Earth come into my circle.

I call upon the guardians of the East, elements of Air bring wisdom to my circle.

I call upon the guardians of the South, elements of Fire to cleanse the spells I cast.

I call upon the guardians of the West, elements of water to purify my deeds. So Mote it be".

Chapter 12: Broomsticks

A Wiccan broomstick is also known as a 'besom'. A besom is a tool used in Wicca to cleanse and purify a space which will be used for a ritual. A traditional Wiccan besom is an ash stave handle with bristles made from birch twigs. The twigs are tied on using thin pieces of willow wood.

While it does not usually touch the ground, a besom is used to "sweep out" the negative energies in a room and is often held a few inches above the ground to do so.

As a tool, the besom is usually thought of as masculine in nature due to its phallic shape and symbolism. However the besom's components are of both masculine and feminine orientation.

The handle, an ash stave, is masculine in nature while the birch used for the bristles is thought of as feminine in nature. The besom is thought to be involved with fairies.

The besom is an important part of Wiccan handfasting ceremonies in some traditions with the couple jumping over the besom during the ceremony.

As an alternative, the couple may jump over a small bonfire.

According to a note in the MacGregor Mather's translation of 'Abramelin', witches mounted upon broomsticks were said to leap around the fields while hallucinating with the aid of the flying ointment, in order to "teach the crops how high to grow", the vivid hallucinatory experience thus caused making them believe that they had flown great distances.

Chapter 13: Divination

There are many different methods of divination that you may choose to use in your magical practice. Some people opt to try many different types, but you may find that you're more gifted in one method than others. Take a look at some of the different methods of divination and see which works best for you and your abilities. And remember, just like with any other skill set, practice makes perfect!

Developing your intuition and psychic abilities

Spend any time at all in the Pagan or Wiccan communities and you're bound to meet individuals who have some fairly pronounced psychic abilities However, many people believe that everyone has some degree of latent psychic abilities. In some people, these abilities tend to manifest in a more obvious manner. In others, it just sits under the surface, waiting to be tapped into. Here are some tips on developing your own psychic gifts and divinatory abilities.

Intuition is the ability to just know things without being told. Many intuitive people make excellent Tarot card readers; because this skill gives them an advantage when reading cards for a client. This is sometimes referred to as *'clairsentience'*. Of all the psychic abilities, intuition may well be the most common.

Tarot card readings

To people unfamiliar with divination, it may seem that someone who reads Tarot cards is "predicting the future." However, most Tarot card readers will tell you that the cards simply offer a guideline, and the reader is simply interpreting the probable outcome based upon the forces presently at work. Think of Tarot as a tool for self-awareness and reflection, rather than "fortune telling."

Tea Leaf Readings

There are numerous methods of divination that people have used since time began. One of the most iconic is the notion of reading tea leaves, also called 'tasseography' or 'tasseomancy'. This divination method isn't quite as ancient as some of the other popular and well-known systems, and appears to have begun around the 17th century.

Pendulums

A pendulum is one of the simplest and easiest forms of divination. It's a simple matter of Yes/No questions being asked and answered. Although you can purchase pendulums commercially, ranging from about £10 - £30, it's not hard to make one of your own.

Typically, most people use a crystal or stone, but you can use any object that's got a bit of weight to it. There are several different ways you can use a pendulum for divination — you'd be surprised what you can learn with "yes" and "no" answers.

The trick is to learn to ask the right questions. Asking a question such as "Am I a boy?" will show you how the pendulum moves for "yes" or "no2"!

Reading the bones

The use of bones for divination, sometimes called *'osteomancy'*, has been performed by cultures throughout the world for millennia. While there are numerous different methods, the primary purpose is the same: to foretell the future using the messages displayed in the bones.

Moon, mirror and water scrying

Are you one of those people who feels more sensitive and alert during the time of the full moon? Channel that energy into something useful, and try this simple yet effective water scrying divination rite. This can be done by looking into something that has a reflection, water, mirror stare into the reflection and see what appears…

Palm readings

This practice has been around for many years typically associated with the gypsy community.

Palm reading involves looking into the palms and reading the lines and marks on a person's hand, to gain insight on their past, present and future.

Whichever means of divination you use, it is important to always cast your circle and call in the four corners,

Never ask disrespectful questions or ask for answers you may not want to hear.

Keep an open mind and do what feels best for you.

Chapter 14: Spells, Tools and Ingredients Needed for Spells

The wonderful thing about magic and Wicca is that there are no strict rules on what you need to do and add to make up a spell. Remember it is your intention and thoughts that make the spells work.

1 . First of all, you need to decide what your spell is going to be for:

- Love, Money, Health, Healing, Protection and so on!

2. You then have to find the ingredients that will help you to make that spell this will normally consist of:

- Herbs
- Crystals
- Candles
- Aromatherapy
- Altar items

3. You then have to blend it all together; it's like adding ingredients to a recipe.

- So you would light your charcoal disc and place it into the cauldron.
- Add your herbs and aromatherapy oil or oils
- You may want to visualise what you want in your head. If you are using a crystal or hoodoo doll you may circle this in the smoke.
- You then chant your spell. Remember it has to rhyme a little bit but don't worry if it doesn't.

An example for a love chant could be:

"In the smoke let me see that my true love comes to me. With this crystal I ask you to bless, so my love will be my best. So mote it be".

You may want to light a candle that represents love and as it burns you may want to chant a love spell as well:
"As I light this candle bright, let true love come into sight. So mote it be".

Chants should always be done three time as this increases the power of three times three.

You would then leave the burned candle wax at the back door and carry the item (eg – crystal, Hoodoo Doll,….) you have used around with you, or put it under your pillow.

You then end your spell session by closing your circle.

It is always good to record your spells in your Book of Shadows.

It is always important to note that your spells will not always work straight away. It may take time for you to see the results. Be patient and persistent.

Your spell will only work if the intention is for your benefit and for the good of others.

What you will comes back on you three times three.

Crossroads

Anything that you need to get rid of that is negative after you have done your spell, for example candle wax, herbs, crystals and hoodoo dolls can be left at a crossroad (where two roads cross over). Place it there and walk away; don't look back.

Chapter 15: Thought Forms

In a lot of spells, you will hear me mention 'thought forms'; these are the keys to your magic.

Using Thought Forms

Thought forms could be thought of as non-physical entities that exist in either the mental or the astral planes. These entities are created solely from thought. Every thought generates vibrations in the mental body, and they may even assume a floating form or take on a colour. Thought forms are sometimes seen by clairvoyants but may also intuitively be sensed by others.

Low natured thoughts like anger, hate, lust, greed, and so on, create thought forms that are dense in colour and form. Thoughts that are more spiritual tend to generate forms possessing a greater purity, clarity, and refinement.

Thought forms can be aimed towards anyone but in order for them to be effective, they must latch onto a similar vibration in the other person's energy or aura. If they are unable to do so, they can come straight back to the sender. This also plays into the theory that whatever you put out into the world comes back, in some way, shape or form. Knowing this, it is virtually impossible to think about what kind of energy you are sending out before you send it. Remember that one who directs evil towards another runs the risk of having it return.

The strength and clarity of the original thought will determine how far it can travel and how strong it is.

Some believe that the thought forms have the capability to assume their own energy and might even appear to be intelligent and independent. Some thought forms may even stay in existence for years, while others can become uncontrollable and turn back on their senders.

Thought forms, are also referred to in magic as '*artificial elements*', which are created though a ritual involving intense concentration, repetition, and visualisation.

Thought forms can be directed towards individuals to protect and heal, or to harm. Thought forms can also be created to perform low-level tasks and errands.

Some thought forms can occur spontaneously, from group thinking or from like-minded people. Whenever a group of people concentrates on the same thought, ideas, or goals, such as a team of employees or a crowd of demonstrators, a group mind occurs. Usually, when the group disbands, the power of the group mind dissipates as well.

The goddess comes in all shapes, sizes and colours, but plays an integral part in the Wiccan way of life.

Chapter 16: Hoodoo Dolls

Now there is a difference between Hoodoo and Voodoo. Hoodoo is used for white magic, so it is good to use a doll to act as a vessel or focal point. You can tell the difference between them as Hoodoo dolls come with a heart on them.

They are easy to make, or you can buy them online or in a magical shop.

The history of Hoodoo dolls spans hundreds of years and they have been used in magical rituals by all walks of life.

If you feel uncomfortable in using a doll then your middle finger can be used to visualise the person or yourself.

Chapter 17: Book of shadows

What is a Book of Shadows?

A Book of Shadows is simply a blank book where you keep track of all your magic items. This might also be called a '*Grimoire*'.

This blank book is a place where you can write down any information you think is interesting or useful to you as Wiccan.

If you are planning on doing rituals, you should probably start your own Book of Shadows so that you can keep track of the work you are doing.

A Book of Shadows can be any sort of book, but it will need to be fairly large because you will be writing a lot of things in it. You could also use a blank sketchbook or even find a nice book at a bookstore or art supply store.

During the Dark Ages in Europe, witches kept a little flame of enlightenment burning, and continued to store their ancient knowledge in their books, despite the risks incurred should the book be discovered. If a witch was indeed caught with a grimoire during the Burning Times, it meant torture and certain death.

A Book of Shadows is a very powerful thing – and it is basically a repository of magic.

The book grows more powerful with each passing year, as you expand it. This is a book that should be handwritten and a book that should always be treated with respect. It is also important to never let anyone else handle your book since it is a sacred and personal item.

A Book of Shadows usually includes:
- Spells
- Rituals
- Prayers
- Magical correspondence
- Information on magic itself
- Incantations
- Pictures or sketches
- Moon or tide charts
- Symbols
- God/Goddess pages
- A coven section
- Records of your magical workings and experiences

You may choose to hide your book away or keep it displayed on your altar You can even cast spells on it if you feel that it is powerful enough.

How to create a Book of Shadows

You can use any type of book you like for your magical work. Every Wiccan should make their own Book of Shadows in whatever way they feel comfortable.

A Book of Shadows is a personal and very sacred tool that contains texts relevant to the craft. If you need some guidelines, the suggestions below might be helpful, but remember there are no hard and fast rules.

What is kept in a Book of Shadows is completely up to you. An average book of shadows might have some common items as you will see below.

Typical Table of Contents

a. The Title – Book of Shadows, with your Magical Name.
b. The Wiccan Rede.
c. A dedication.
d. Tools and altar layout.
e. Circle casting procedures.
f. Deities.
g. Rituals, spells and potions.
h. Herbal remedies.
i. Symbols and magical alphabet.
j. Stones, crystals and gems.
k. The Moon cycle.
l. Esbats.
m. Sabbats.
n. Divination tools like tarot or the pendulum.
o. Candle magic.
p. Anything you want, need or desire!

Different ways to have your Book of Shadows

Having an E-Book of Shadows

In this digital age, almost everything is digitalised. If you do plan on using a computer to store your work, it is important to keep a few things in mind.
- While a computer is a very handy tool for recording information, you should keep a copy of all your files in case you lose your (laptop) computer or it gets infected with a virus.
- If you are using a shared computer, secure your documents with a password that must be entered upon opening the document.
- While an E-book has lots of advantages having a computer while performing a ritual is rather impractical unless you are using a tablet or laptop.

A Binder
Another popular way to keep a Book of Shadows is to use a binder. A binder allows you to organise your pages in the exact order you want them to be.

A Notebook
If you do not feel like having an e-Book of Shadows or a binder, you can also use a notebook. Having a notebook is very practical. The only disadvantage is that space is more limited.

A Handmade Book of Shadows
If you are very creative and have enough time, you can also make a Book of Shadows that is completely handmade.

Chapter 18: Mojo Bags

Mojo Bags are also called *spell bags, medicine bags, charm bags, gris-gris bags, prayer bags,* and *amulets*.
Traditional Mojo Bags originated in Africa and are integrated with the folk magic Hoodoo. In modern Wicca, the bags are given names. They are regularly fed (blessed or empowered) and maintained.

What are Mojo Bags?
Mojo Bags are small bags that are worn or kept somewhere personal such as under a pillow or on an altar, that have been filled with a mix of specifically chosen items to help achieve a desired result.

How do you make a Mojo Bag?
Start with a small, lovely bag, which you can either make yourself or buy. If you are going to make it yourself, choose a soft, natural material; cotton, hemp or felt are all excellent.

Either cut the material into two pieces of a desired shape and sew them together leaving an opening, or simply use a square or circle of the fabric, that you will place your items in the centre of, and tie tightly when you have finished.

Set an intention

- Identify what the bag is for ~ love, luck, money, protection, safe travels?

- Choose the items to go into your bag, based upon your intention. Each item should have its own purpose and should also support your overall intention.

- For love you might choose a rose quartz crystal, a heart shaped charm, some dried rose petals, a written intention or name, and a few sprigs of dried lavender.

- For protection you might choose a small piece of obsidian, some frankincense, black beans, a silver charm that you feel affords you protection, and a pinch of fennel or elder.

- Other items might include stones, shells, herbs, crystals, good luck charms, coins, stone or wood carvings, leaves or feathers.

- Fill your bag with an odd number of items (at least three).

- Visualise your intention very clearly as you put each item in your Mojo Bag.

When your bag is full of your items, wind a cord around the open end several times, with enough length left that you can wear it around your neck if that is what you wish to do. Otherwise you can tuck or pin it into any part of your clothing.

Say an incantation, prayer, or spoken intention over your Mojo Bag to lock in your energy.

Light some incense (I use white sage) and pass your bag through the smoke several times to purify the contents. Again, state your intention with clarity and vision.

Folk magick is based upon the idea that everything is alive, i.e. everything has a rhythm and an energy.

If you do not keep infusing your intention into something, the contents will not hold your energy. So, for the lifetime of your Mojo Bag, keep setting your intention and locking in your energy, as identified above.
You may wish to do this as a ritual, say once per week, or simply anytime the inclination takes you.

Now is a good time to have a little break and a cup of tea or coffee.

Chapter 19: Wiccan Ways to Use Herbs

Herbs are used in magical rituals and spells for their "vibrations" or "essences". Herbs, like people, actually have gender, and they are ruled by a planet, an element, and are often sacred to a God or Goddess.

The use of herbs in Wicca is known as 'herbal correspondence'. The use of herbs is a key element to Wiccan magic and spells. Growing and nurturing herbs in your own magical garden is a wonderful way to gain an advantage because you can nurture the herbs with your love and compassion.

A plant will then have all of the influence of the sun and fire, along with your own personal energies. Whether you use herbs in charms and sachets, as incense or in baths, is your own personal choice.

Charms and Sachets – Simple fill a small bag, of the correct colour or material, with herbs to make a charm or sachet. You can then carry the charm with you, put it under your pillow, hang it in the house or car, or bury or burn it, depending on the purpose and the spell you are performing.

Incense – Herbs can be used in incense and burned as part of a ritual such as using a sage smudge to clear negative vibrations from a space.

Bath – Using herbs in the bath is also a great way to utilise them. You can make a sachet and place it in your ritual or healing bath. Soothing herbs like lavender make a very relaxing bath, and you can use certain herbs to alleviate skin and other conditions, such as using eucalyptus in a bath when you have a cold or flu.

Oils – You can also place herbs in an oil and let them steep for a few days, then strain them. Anointing oils can be used for your ritual work, as beauty oils for your hair, skin and nails. Oils like jojoba work well for this.

Teas - Using herbs for teas is a wonderful way to heal the body from the inside out. Some herbs can also be used to mildly alter consciousness, such as valerian or kava kava, which can facilitate a beautiful relaxing and trance like state.

Smoking – Some herbs can also be smoked, if desired. You can make herbal smoking mixtures, which will also facilitate altered states of consciousness.

In rituals and spells, herbs can be sprinkled or simply placed around or within boundaries, or even around the home.

Herbs and plants should always be used with great care and respect. There is no such thing as a weed because every plant has a purpose in life.

Dandelion, for example, has many amazing healing and nutritional qualities, which are extremely beneficial to both wildlife and people. You can find herbs growing wild, and even in the city, and you gather herbs and use them with love in your heart.

Remember you do not have to get every single herb as this will then become very expensive: Start by getting the most popular ones that you can see being used in the spells in this book, and then you can build them up as you become more experienced.

ANGELICA ROOT: Sun, fire, masculine

Angelica root can be used as protection and exorcism licence. You can also carry the root in a pouch as a protective talisman. Added to a bath, it can remove hexes. Smoking the leaves may cause visions.

- Angelica root protects by the creation of a barrier against negative energy, filling the user with positive energy.
- It can be used to remove curses, hexes, or spells that have been cast against you.
- Angelica root enhances your aura, and gives you a joyful outlook
- Angelica root relieves tension headaches, acts as a diuretic, is beneficial to the stomach and digestion.
- It can also relieve build-up of phlegm due to asthma and bronchitis. Always use with caution as large doses can negatively affect blood pressure, heart, and respiration. If pregnant, it can cause miscarriage.

BASIL: Mars, Fire, Masculine

- Can be used for love and prosperity root.
- Can be carried to attract wealth.
- Sprinkle basil over your sleeping lover to assure fidelity.
- Use it in a ritual bath to bring new love in or to free yourself of an old love.
- Also used for purification baths. Sprinkle on the floor for protection and burn as an exorcism incense.

BAY LEAVES: Sun, Fire, Masculine

- Used in potions for visions, clairvoyance and wisdom.
- Placed under your pillow, it can induce prophetic dreams. The priestesses at Delphi are said to have chewed bay leaves to induce their visions and prophesies.
- Carried, it can ward off evil.

- Scatter or burn for exorcism. Scatter on the floor, and then sweep out for protection.
- Can be added to cleansing teas and baths.

BURDOCK: Venus, Water, Feminine
- Used in protection incenses and for healing, especially the feet.
- Carry as a protection sachet or burn for purification of a room.
- Rinse with a root decoction for ridding oneself of a gloomy feeling about yourself or others.

BRAMBLE (BLACKBERRY) LEAF: Venus, Water, Feminine
- Bramble is a powerful herb of protection, and it can be used in invocations to the goddess Brigit, who presides over healing, poetry, sacred wells and smithcraft.
- Also use to attract wealth.
- If twined into a wreath with rowan and ivy, it will keep away evil spirits.
- Also can be used to invoke and attract faeries spirits.

CAMELLIA: Moon, Water, Feminine
- Brings riches and luxury, expresses gratitude.
- Place fresh blossoms in water on an alter during a ritual to attract money and prosperity.
- Used in traditional Chinese medicine for treating skin conditions.

CARAWAY: Mercury, Air, Masculine
- Carry for protection against spirits who mean to harm, especially Lilith.
- The seeds can be used to ensure faithfulness, and can be used in spells to attract a lover. Used in cooking, will induce lust.

CATNIP: Water, Venus, Feminine
- Catnip can be used in animal magic and for healing pets, increases psychic bond with animals.
- Use as a tea for happiness and relaxation.
- Can also be used during mediation, increases psychic abilities.
- Useful in love magic – try burning dried leaves for love wishes.

CAYENNE PEPPER: Mars, Fire, Masculine
- Used in hexes or to break a hex. Used in love or separation spells.
- The fire or spark of the spirit adds power to any spell. Contains capsaicin, which acts as a stimulating digestive aid. Apply externally for joint pain.
- Aids circulation, blood pressure, and colds. Those with ulcers or chronic bowel disorders should avoid using in large quantities.
-

CEDAR: Sun, Fire, Masculine
- Used for healing, purification, money, protection and love.
- Cedar smoke is purifying and can cure nightmares.
- Keep cedar in your wallet or purse to attract money, and use in money incense.
- It can also be used in love sachets or burned to induce psychic powers. Use to draw Earth energy and grounding.

CINNAMON: Sun, Fire, Masculine
- Used for spirituality, success, healing, psychic, lust, protection, love.
- Burn cinnamon as an incense or use in sachets and spells for healing, money-drawing, psychic powers, and protection.
- Mix with frankincense, myrrh and sandalwood for a strong protection incense to be burned every day. Also a male aphrodisiac.

CLOVES: Jupiter, Fire, Masculine
- Protection, exorcism, love, money, good luck.
- Use incense to attract money, drive away negativity, purify, gain luck or stop gossip.
- Wear to attract the opposite sex or for protection. Worn or carried to repel negative energies around you. Also said to protect babies in their cots if hung over them strung together.

COLTSFOOT: Venus, Water, Feminine
- Add to love sachets and use in spells for peace and tranquillity.
- Smoke the leaves to aid obtaining visions.
- Also a soothing expectorant and anti-spasmodic, which can be used to treat bronchitis, whooping cough, asthma, and chronic emphysema.
- Caution: Do not use if pregnant or nursing.

CUMIN: Mars, Fire, Masculine
- Burn with frankincense for protection.
- Mix with salt and scatter to keep away evil spirits and bad luck.
- Use in love spells. Steep cumin seed in wine to induce lust.
- Place the seeds on, in or near an object to prevent theft. Burn with frankincense for protection.

RED CLOVER: Mercury, Air, Masculine
- Use for protection, money, love, fidelity, exorcism, success, clairvoyance and beauty.
- Brings good luck. Induces clairvoyant powers.
- Used for rituals to enhance beauty and youth.

COMFREY LEAF: Air, Saturn, feminine
- A strong herb protection against any type of negativity, especially when travelling, and particularly for protection in the astral realms.
- Very nutritious, beneficial for healing sprains, strains, fractures and sores. Also soothes an upset stomach.

DILL: Mercury, Fire, Masculine
- Hang in the doorway to protect your home, or carry to protect your person. Can be used in money spells.
- Add to ritual bath to become irresistible to the one you desire. Used in love and lust spells.

DANDELION LEAF: Jupiter, Air, Masculine
- Used for divination, wishes and calling spirits.
- The root can be used in a tea to enhance psychic powers.
- Used in Samhain rituals. Sleep, protection, healing.
- A very nutritious and universally beneficial herb. Use in dream pillows and sachets, the leaves and flowers can be used in tea for healing.

EUCALYPTUS LEAF: Air, Moon, Feminine
- Uses include great healing properties, killing germs, infections, easing lung congestion, heart stimulant. Attracts healing vibrations and protection.
- Use to purify and cleanse any space of unwanted energies. Also useful in dream and sleep pillows.

FENNEL SEED: Mercury, Fire, Masculine
- Used for healing, longevity, courage, vitality and strength.
- Used for protection spells of all kinds. Prevents curses, possession and negativity. Use for purification.
- Gives strength, courage and longevity. Delicious flavour, purifies breath, aids digestion and weight-loss.

FEVERFEW: Venus, Water, Feminine
- Used for love and protection.
- Include in charms or sachets. Also a strong herb for health and spiritual healing.
- Used to ward off sickness and bolster immune system. Protects travellers – keep in your suitcase or car next time you travel.
- Excellent treatment for migraine headaches – eases inflammation and constriction of the blood vessels in the head, reduces sensitivity to light and nausea.

FLAX SEED: Mercury, Fire, Masculine
- Used to keep the peace at home – placed in a bowl it can help absorb negative energy. Useful in healing and protection spells.
- You can carry flax seeds in your wallet or purse to attract money.
- Very nutritional, good for cholesterol.

GARLIC: Mars, Fire, Masculine
- Used in protection spells, traditionally used to ward off vampires. Great healing properties, antiviral, antifungal, strengthening.
- The ancient Greeks placed garlic on the stone cairns at crossroads as an offering to Hecate.

GINGER: Mars, Fire, Masculine
- Used to attract love, money, success and power.
- Used in love spells. Eat before performing spells to increase your power.

GINSENG POWDER: Sun, Fire, Masculine
- Used for rejuvenation, longevity and sexual potency.
- Use the root in spells to attract love, maintain health, draw money and ensure sexual potency.
- Carry to enhance beauty.
- Burn to break curses or ward off evil spirits.
- Make into a lust enhancing tea.
- Useful as an antidepressant, equalises pressure and aids digestion.

HIBISCUS FLOWER: Venus, Water, Feminine
- Useful as an aphrodisiac and in love spells. Also used to induce dreams, and enhance psychic ability and divination.
- Soothes nerves, antispasmodic.
- Tea aids digestion, and sweetens breath.
- Helpful with itchy skin.

HOLLY LEAF: Mars, Fire, Masculine
- Used to increase luck and enhance dreams and magic.
- An excellent protective herb, keeps away lightening, poison, evil spirits, and other malign forces.
- The wood is used for all magical tools, as it will enhance any wish you have.
- A powerful protection.
- Do not consume, for ritual use only.

HOPS: Mars, Air, Masculine
- Used in healing incenses and spells. Put inside pillow to induce sleep.
- Tea helps with restful sleep. Also, drink tea after magical practices to balance and refocus your energy back to ordinary reality.
- Used in healing sachets and amulets.
- Also burn during healing prayers.

HOREHOUND: Mercury, Earth, Masculine
- Used as a tea to increase energy and strength, both physically and mentally.
- It also increases concentration and focus.
- Carry or burn for protection wishes.
- Called the "seed of Horus" by the ancient Egyptians, it is excellent for blessing one's home. Gather flowering Horehound and tie with a ribbon, then hang in your home to keep it free of negative energy.
- The leaves and stems are used in sweets, cough drops, and syrups. It is used to treat asthma, coughs, colds, bronchitis, sore throats, and skin irritations. Also used as a diaphoretic, diuretic, expectorant, laxative, stimulant and stomachic.

HYSSOP: Jupiter, Fire, Masculine
- An excellent purifying herb and used in purification baths and spells.
- Associated with serpents and dragons, and can be burned as an incense to call on dragon energy. Aids in physical and spiritual protection.

JUNIPER BERRIES: Sun, Fire, Masculine
- Useful for protection magic of all kinds.
- Makes a nice incense for protection. It can be burned or carried to enhance psychic powers. Attracts good, healthy energies and love.
- Aids in digestion, intestinal cramps, diuretic, eases arthritis. Banishes energies injurious to good health.

MANDRAKE ROOT: Mercury, Fire, Masculine
- Used for protection, love, money, fertility and health.
- Mandrake intensifies the magic of any spell. To charge mandrake root with your personal power, sleep with it for 3 nights during a full moon.
- A hallucinogen when used in tea – it has great power as a visionary herb, empowering your visions and propelling them into manifestation.
- A whole mandrake root placed in the home will bring prosperity and protection.
- Carried it will attract love and courage.

MORNING GLORY BLOSSOMS: Neptune, Water, Masculine
- Promotes happiness, peace and visions.
- Place under your pillow to stop nightmares and induce beneficial psychic dreams.
- Sacred to the Aztecs.
- Do not consume – TOXIC.

MOSS: Jupiter, Earth, Masculine
- To ensure good luck, especially with money, carry any type of moss removed from a gravestone.
- Used in prosperity spells. Gnome magic and spells to Mother Earth.
- Place in your bra when a male lover is near to attract sexual attention.

MUGWORT: Venus, Earth, Feminine
- Used in dream pillows for prophetic dreams.
- Burn with sandalwood or wormwood for scrying rituals.
- Drink as a tea sweetened with honey before divination.
- The plain tea can also be used to wash crystal balls and magic mirrors. Leaves of mugwort can be placed around these to aid in scrying.

NETTLES: Mars, Fire, Masculine
- Carry to remove a curse and send it back, or sprinkle around the house to keep out evil.
- Used in purification baths. Highly nutritious for anaemia, skin disorders and allergies, restores health, expectorant, stops bleeding.
- One of the nine sacred herbs of the Anglo-Saxons.

NUTMEG: Jupiter, Fire, Masculine
- Used for luck, money and health.
- Carry for good luck and to strengthen clairvoyant powers.
- Used in money and prosperity spells.
- Hallucinogen when made into a tea.
- TOXIC in large doses! Take no more than a pinch!

PASSION FLOWER: Venus, Water, Feminine
- Promotes emotional balance, peace, attracts friendship and prosperity.
- Heightens libido, use in love spells.
- Calming and soothing, Promotes emotional balance, aid in sleep.
- Use to relieve nerve pain and hysteria.

PEPPERMINT: Mercury, Fire, Masculine
- Used for purification, sleep, love, healing and psychic powers.
- Promotes sleep and visionary dreams. Used in healing and purification baths. Burn as a winter incense.
- Very useful for stomach upset, heartburn, nausea, and to ease congestion during colds and flu.

PINE: Sun, Air, Masculine
- Used to promote sacred wisdom, prosperity, fertility and healing. The pine tree is an evergreen, its old title was "the sweetest of woods". Its needles are valuable source of vitamin C and can loosen a tight chest.
- The scent of pine is useful in the alleviation of guilt. Burn for strength, and to reverse negative energies.

RASPBERRY LEAF: Venus, Water, Feminine
- Used to protection, healing and love. Calming, promotes sleep and visions.
- Useful during pregnancy and childbirth, eases diarrhoea, nausea and vomiting and is beneficial to the kidneys.

ROSE PETALS: Venus, Water, Feminine
- Used for love, psychic powers, healing, luck and protection.
- Used in love spells of all kinds. Drink rose tea before bed for prophetic dreams.
- Domestic peace and happiness, promotes joy of giving. Helps clear away headaches, dizziness, mouth sores and menstrual cramps.
- Heart and nerve tonic

ROSE HIPS: Venus, Water, Feminine
- Rose hips are very high in vitamin C. Rose hips also contain A,B,E and K, organic acids and pectin, and have a high concentration of iron.
- The hips are strung like beads and worn to attract love. A woman should eat rose hips during her menstrual cycle. A woman's lover should gather roses for this purpose. The earliest known gardening was the planting of roses along the most travelled routes of early nomadic humans.

ROSEMARY: Sun, Fire, Masculine
- Used for protection, love, lust, mental powers, exorcism, purification, healing, sleep and youth.
- Burned to purify and cleanse. Used in love and lust incense and potions. Used for healing of all kinds. A tea of rosemary causes the mind to be alert.
- Circulatory, digestive and nerve stimulant.
- Heals headache, depression, and halitosis.

SAGE: Jupiter, Air, Masculine
- Used for immortality, longevity, wisdom, protection and prosperity.
- Used in healing and money spells.
- Purifying, use as incense during sacred rituals – walk the smoke to the four corners of the room to repel and rid negative energies and influences. Especially good when moving into a new home.
- Heals wounds, aids digestion, eases muscle and joint pain, colds and fever.

SALT: Saturn, Earth, Masculine
- Used for prosperity, protection, purification, consecration of ritual tools.
- Sprinkle a few grains around your sacred space to clear it of any unpleasant presences. Some ancient rituals call for the pouring of dry salt into a receptacle of water to symbolise the dissolving of evil.

SEAWEED: Moon, Water, Feminine
- Offers protection to those at sea. Summons sea spirits and sea winds.
- Used in sachets and spells to increase psychic powers. Scrub the floors and doors of a business with an infusion to attract customers and bring in positive energy.
- Used in money spells. Fill a small jar with whiskey, add kelp, close cap tightly and place in a kitchen window. Ensures a steady flow of money into the household.
- Helps regulate an underactive thyroid.
- Relieves the pain of rheumatism and rheumatic joints.

ST JOHNS WORT: Sun, Fire, Masculine
- Used for health, protection, strength, love, divination, happiness and exorcism.
- A druid sacred herb. Used in protection and exorcism spells and incense of all kinds.
- Used as a tea to treat depression.
- Use the leaves in a necklace to ward off sickness and tension.
- Carry to strengthen your courage and conviction.
- Burn to banish, negative thoughts and energies.

STAR ANISE: Jupiter, Air, Masculine
- Used for protection, purification, youth, psychic powers and luck.
- Also used for meditation and psychic power incenses. Can be used in purification baths. Wards off evil and averts the evil eye.
- A pillow stuffed with star anise seeds keep away nightmares. The tree is planted by the Japanese around temples and on graves as an herb of consecration and protection.
- The seeds make excellent pendulums.
- The tree is often grown near Buddhist temples where it is revered.
- A stimulant and diuretic. Promotes digestion and relieves flatulence.

TEA: Sun, Fire, Masculine
- Signifies riches, courage and strength.
- Use the leaves in money sachets, incense and spells. A stimulant. Green tea is rich in antioxidants, and other youth enhancing compounds. The leaves can be used in scrying.

TOBACCO LEAF: Mars, Fire, Masculine
- Sacred to the Native American tradition. Tobacco ties – wrap tobacco leaves in pieces of white, red, yellow and black cloth, and hang them around the ceremonial space at the four cardinal directions.
- Smoke to allow communication with spirits. Burn as an incense to purify a space. Spirits appreciate offerings of tobacco.

THISTLE FLOWER: Mars, Fire, Masculine
- Represents courage defence and deep-rooted ideals.
- Protection spells, also used to bring spiritual and financial blessings.
- Carry in an amulet for joy, energy, vitality, and protection.
- Can be burned as an incense for protection and to also counteract hexing.

THYME: Venus, Water, Feminine
- Burn for good health and use in healing spells.
- Burn as purification incense.
- Wear to increase psychic powers.

VALERIAN ROOT: Venus, Water, Feminine
- A muscle relaxant and a tranquiliser. Used for dream magic and sleep protection baths.
- Keep in the home or grow in the garden too aid in keeping harmony.
- Maybe used to purify a ritual space. Useful in consecrating incense burners.
- Drink tea daily, in moderate doses, during times of purification.

VANILLA: Venus, Water, Feminine
- Use to attract love, enhance seduction and mental powers.
- Used in love sachets, and wear the fragrant oil as an aphrodisiac.

WILLOW BARK: Moon, Water, Feminine
- Used for love, divination, protection and healing.
- Can carry and use in spells to attract love.
- Use the leaves, bark and wood in healing spells.
- Eases muscle and joint pain, beneficial for arthritis.

YARROW FLOWER: Venus, Water, Feminine
- Used to dispel melancholy, negative energy, lingering sorrow, or depression.
- Can be carried as a sachet or amulet it repels or rids of negative influences. Aids in divination. Good remedy for colds.
- Opens the pores and purifies the blood. Said to prevent baldness as a hair wash.

Wiccan Herbs quick reference

Barberry Root: Protection, Luck, Prosperity, Power

Catnip: Friendship, Happiness, Psychic Dreams

Chamomile; Sleep, Meditation, Money, Love, Peace

Clove: Protection, Love, Abundance

Dandelion: Divination, Wishes, Love, Abundance

Goat's Rue: Healing, Health, Heal a broken heart

Hibiscus: Love, Lust, Divination to see sprits

Hops Strobile: Healing, Sleep, Dream work

Lavender: Relaxation, Sleep, Love, Peace

Liquorice: Love, Lust, Fidelity

Milk Thistle: Protection, Strength, Hex-Breaking

Mint: Protection, Healing, Money

Mugwort: Strength, Psychic Powers, Protection, Prophetic Dreams, Healing, Astral Projection, Cleansing & Feminine Energy

Nettle: Exorcism, Protection, Healing

Nutmeg: Luck, Money, Health, Fidelity

Passion Flower: Peace, Sleep, Friendship, Love, Calm

Rose: Love, Healing, Protection, Luck

Rosehip: Love, Healing, Luck, Protection

Rosemary: Banish Negativity, Cleansing

Sage: Wisdom, Protection, Wishes

Wormwood: Protection, Love, Divination, Meditation

Yarrow: Courage, Love, Divination, Happiness

Resins

There are lots of different types of resins that are available.

These are usually for mixing with herbs to burn on your charcoal bricks in your cauldron. They can be used to enhance your spells or just used when you are doing meditation and healing work.

"Mother Earth gives us everything we need, let us nurture and protect her".

Wiccan Herbs a wonderful and perfect gift to us all

Chapter 20: Candle Magic

Candle magic has been used for centuries and can be used as part of your spell. Choose the colour candle that matches your spell light it and chant your spell.

You can also anoint your candle with oil. Choose the oil that matches your spell.

To bring something to you (for example, love), put a drop of oil on each end of the candle. Rub the oil in at both ends working inwards. To send things away from you, put a few drops of oil in the middle of the candle and rub the oil from the middle in an outwards direction.

Remember to chant what you want the candle to do.

RED - Desire, Energy, Strength, Courage

ORANGE - Ambition, Luck Encouragement

PURPLE - Psychic ability, Spiritual Power

YELLOW - Happiness, Creativity, Confidence

BLUE - Wisdom, Dreams, Inspiration

GREEN - Success, Prosperity, Fertility

WHITE - Enlightenment, Healing, Cleansing

BLACK - Banishing, Protection, Negativity

Chapter 21: Crystals

Amethyst: Protection, Stress Relief, Disperses Negative Energies

Black Obsidian: Grounding, Protection, Healing

Bloodstone: Seeing Things Through, Staying True To Oneself

Citrine: Confidence, Happiness, Strength

Clear Quartz: Healing, Clarity, Creativity

Green Aventurine: Luck, Healing, Imagination

Lapis Lazuli: Wisdom, Intuition, Clarity

Red Carnelian: Confidence, Empowerment, Physical Vitality

Rose Quartz: Love, Harmony, Peace

Sodalite: Rationality, Truth, Intuition

Tiger's Eye: Protection, Personal Power, Determination

Yellow Jasper: Protection, Boosts Positivity, Health

Chapter 22: Aromatherapy Oils

Basil: Uplifting, Energising, Purifying

Chamomile: Relaxing, Calming, Revitalising

Eucalyptus: Revitalising, Invigorating, Clarifying

Frankincense: Relaxing, Focusing, Centering

Ginger: Balancing, Clarifying, Stabilizing

Lavender: Soothing, Normalising, Balancing

Lemon: Refreshing, Cheerful, Uplifting

Orange: Refreshing, Uplifting, Invigorating

Patchouli: Romantic, Soothing, Stimulating

Rose: Love, Healing, Protection, Luck

Sage: Normalising, Balancing, Soothing

Ylang Ylang: Soothing, Romantic, Comforting

These are just some of the most popular and easy to find ingredients.

Chapter 23: Spell Directory

In this section I have put together a number of different spells that you can start using straight away. I have chosen ingredients that are easy to find and simple to use. Saying what you are adding to the caldron will enhance your spell (eg, "*I add Sage*")

You may want to try these at first and as you gain in experience you can then start to make up your own.

You will notice that there are gaps at the end of the spells. This is for you to write in notes, ideas or feelings you have while performing thee spells.

You can also add notes to these spells when you copy them into your own Book of Shadows.

Simple Love Spell

Ingredients
Rose Herb

Chamomile Herb

Lavender Herb

Rose Quartz Crystal

Light your charcoal.
- Sprinkle the herbs into the charcoal and hold your crystal over the smoke and think about the one you love (be realistic).
- Chant the following: "I *call upon Eros to bring to me the true love I seek.*
- *Help clear my vision so i see what this love has in store for me.*
- *With a picture so clear in my mind this I bind, to bring my true love for me to find. So mote it be*".
- Now place some of the herbs into your pouch and with the crystal and keep this under your pillow or bed.

Always remember that you cannot force someone to love you. You should never seek someone else love. Remember the laws of the three times three.

Love spell 2

Ingredients
Rose Herb

Chamomile Herb

Lavender Herb

Hoodoo Doll

- Light your charcoal.
- Sprinkle the herbs onto the charcoal and hold your hoodoo doll over the smoke.
- Circle clockwise.
- Chant the following:

    "In my dreams bring to me the one that has been made for me.
    Help me be where i need to be so my true love can find me.
    Help me determine accurately the difference between love and lust.
    And there for being to the love I can truly trust.
    So mote it be."
- Hold the doll in both hands like you are praying then close your eyes and say, *"3 times 3 let it be"*.

Sock Protection Spell

Ingredients
Hawthorn Berry

Camomile Herb

Resin

Lavender

- Light cauldron and add the resin and herbs
- Circle the sock around the smoke.
- Chant the following "*Come to me protection thee. Protect my home three time three. Keep from me those who wish me harm protection comes in this, magic charm So mote it be*".
- Place some of each of the herbs and resin to the sock and tie.
- Again, circle the sock around the smoke and repeat the chant above 3 times.

Pentagram Healing Spell

Ingredients
Hoodoo doll
Lavender oil
Smudge Stick
Pentagram
Feather or Hand

- Light the cauldron and add the lavender oils.
- Gently breathe in through your nose and imagine the smoke healing your mind.
- Hold the hoodoo doll over the smoke and imagine the doll as yourself or the person you want to heal.
- Chant the following.
- *"Bring healing three times three to this doll that represents me (or the name of the person). Cleanse my body of all that ails me. Make me clean three times three. So mote it be".*
- Place the doll one the pentagram and light the sage stick.
- Circle the smoke clockwise while waving it away from you with a feather or hand and chant the following: *"Elements of Earth ground me be. Elements of Air set me free. Elements of Fire cleanse me be. Elements of Water purify me. Spirit, bring unto thee the elements three time three. So mote it be."*
- Place the doll next to your bed to heal or give to the person you want to heal.

Crystal Ball Spell

Ingredients
Crystal Ball

Mugwort

Purple Candle

- Cast your circle and call the four corners.
- Put the mugwort into the cauldron and light the purple candle.
- Close your eyes and put a thought form about connecting yourself to spirit.
- Chant the following: "*Spirit be spirit see, show me what I need to see. Help me receive the message I need to hear and give to it others to bring good cheer. So mote it be*".
- Now looking over at the person you are reading for, close your eyes and concentrate on receiving the message.
- Cup your hands in front of the ball and then look into the ball,
- Remember that the vision does not always show in the ball but sometimes comes in your thoughts.

(A thought form is a vision you manifest in your mind of what you want)

Connect With the Spirit Of a Love One

Ingredients
Bell

Amethyst Point

Rose Herb

Hops

Barberry Root

Purple or Blue Hoodoo Doll

2 Purple Candles

- Cast a circle and call the four corners
- Put the herbs into the cauldron and light the 2 purple candles.
- Close your eyes and put a thought form about connecting yourself to spirit you want to connect to.
- Ring the bell and call the spirit you want to bring in.
- Say "*I call on the spirit of* .... come forward and connect with me."
- Hold the Amethyst over the smoke circle around the smoke and chant the following: "*Protect me and support me to help me communicate.*"
- Hold the hoodoo doll in both hands and think of the person you want to communicate with and chant: "*Hoodoo doll act as a conduit for me bring in spirit that I want to see. Give to me the guidance I need and watch over me as I go forward with this spell. So mote it be.*"
- Keep the doll next to your bed at night.

Financial Gain Spell

Ingredients

Green candle

Green Crystal

Yellow Candle

Sage

Mugwort

Lavender

Bell

Pentagram

- Cast a circle and call the four corners.
- Add your herbs to the charcoal and chant the following while holding your hand over the smoke 3 times.
- Put down your pentagram in front of cauldron and chant "*I call onto thee to bring blessing to me to help secure finance to me. Help me to receive what I need and also to give some to others to mote it be.*"
- Ring the bell and say "*spirit let it be*".
- Light the yellow candle and chant the following: "*Elements of Earth Air Fire and Water bring me the happiness I need so I can help others in my magical deeds. So mote it be*".
- Ring the bell and say "*spirit let it be*".

- Write a very specific goal for this money spell into your piece of paper. Be very clear on the amount you'd like to come into your life and make it an amount that you can actually see coming to you right now.
- Repeat the petition three times in writing then pass the paper over the incense before placing the petition underneath the green candle to be burned.
- Light the green candle and chant the following: *"Hear my plea three times three bring the finances that need."*
- Ring the bell and say *"spirit let it be"*.

Healing Broken House Spell

Ingredients
Tigers Eye Crystal

Sage Stick

Lavender

Mugwort

Bell

- Cast a circle and call the four corners.
- Add your herbs to the charcoal and chant the following while holding your hand over the smoke 3 times: *"Heal this house as it is broken see, Heal all the lives here three times three Oh gods and Goddesses bring to thee the healing this house needs three times three. Negative vibes take please away bring happiness and laughter and fun to stay.*
- *So note it be".*
- Light the candle and imagine the badness being taken away in the light and then chant the verse above again.
- Keep the crystal in your home and put candle wax at the back door.

Positive Relationship Spell

Ingredients
Red Candle

Two Hoodoo Dolls

Rose Dilute Oil

Rose Petals

Red Ribbon

- Cast your circle and call your four corners.
- Then light your cauldron.
- Inscribe the initials for the two people you want to bless into the red candle.
- Add two drops of rose dilute oil to anoint the candle.
- Get your two hoodoo dolls and bind them together (start from the middle of the candle and rub outwards) with the ribbon while saying:
- *"With every moment, love shall grow within me. Radiate from me. Flow towards me. This is my will. So mote it be"*.
- Add the rose petals to your cauldron and hold the bound hoodoo dolls over the smoke whilst thinking of what it is that you desire from this spell.
- Light the candle on a Friday or a full moon and let it burn away completely.

Love potion

Ingredients
Red Candle

Patchouli Oil

Vegetable/Olive Oil

Glass Bottle

Cauldron Kit

White Sage

- Cast the circle and call upon your four corners.
- Light the cauldron.
- Anoint candle with patchouli oil from the outside inwards.
- Add the white sage to the cauldron and chant: *"Bless be tonight. Bring my true love to sight. Bring me the love I seek. To help me fulfil my loves desire. A love to me that will not tyre. So mote it be"*.
- Add a small amount of vegetable/olive oil to the glass bottle.
- Add a few drops of patchouli oil into the bottle.
- Sprinkle the white sage and mix well by placing the lid on top and shaking the bottle.
- Add more sage to the cauldron and hold the bottle over the smoke.
- Thought form your love and desire as you do this chant your spell and again three times and thank spirit.
- Then, pour the oil over the doorstep of the person you love and then over the front of your own doorstep.

Mojo Love Bag

Ingredients

Bag

Sage

Rose Quartz

Patchouli Oil

Passionflower

- Cast your circle and call upon the four corners.
- Light your cauldron and ass sage. Open your bag and add the following:
    - Rose Quartz, Sage, 10 drops of Patchouli oil and Passionflower.
- Hold the bag over the cauldron smoke and tie it three times while chanting: *"Magic love bag bring to me the person that is meant for me. Bind this love forever more to bring the one that I adore.*
So mote it be".
- Keep your mojo bag in your home or give it to the one that you love.

Astral Travel Spell

Ingredients

Black candle

Basil Oil

Dream Tea

Hoodoo Dolls

- Cast your circle and call upon the four corners.
- Anoint the black candle with basil oil from the middle outwards.
- Then light the candle and say: *"Light my way to the path I need to find, keep away badness and dispel it from my mind. So mote it be."*
- Light your cauldron and hold your hoodoo doll over it while chanting the following: *"Love the light fill this doll with might, protect me through my flight. So mote it be".*
- Add the dream tea into the cauldron and hold the hoodoo doll over the smoke.
- Chant the spell again and leave the doll by your bedside when you go to sleep.

Binding Spell

Ingredients
White candle or Hoodoo doll

Red Ribbon

Rosemary Herb

Sage Herb

Basil Oil

- Cast your circle and call your four corners.
- Light your cauldron and add a pinch of sage to cleanse the space.
- On the white candle inscribe who or what you want binding (alternatively you can write on a piece of paper then place it inside the hoodoo doll).
- Get your basil oil and anoint the candle or hoodoo doll with two drops rubbing from the edges inwards while saying the following incantation three times: "*I bind you (person name) from doing harm against other people and harm against yourself. So mote it be*".
- Put rosemary in the cauldron and hold the candle or hoodoo doll over the smoke while envisioning the person you desire to be bound.
- At night bury the candle or hoodoo doll in the ground.

Heal a Broken Heart Spell

Ingredients

2 red candles

Sage

Resin

Lavender oil

Hoodoo Doll

- Cast your circle and call the four corners.
- Light your charcoal and add the Sage and the resin. Remember you can say, "*I add Sage. I add resin*".
- Hold the hoodoo doll above the smoke and chant the following spell:
- "*Heal this broken heart of mine. Help it mend as loves untwine. Give to me the strength I need to be strong. Bring to my heart healing and hear my song. So mote it be*"
- Anoint the candle with lavender oil from the out sides in and focus your mind on the image of your heart healing.
- Light the candle and chant the spell 3 times: "*Bring light back to my heart as my love departs. Heal what is left as we I move forward. Bring blessings and light to all involved so we move on and never unfold. So mote it be*"
- Keep the hoodoo doll close to your heart when you are feeling low.
- Put the left over wax at your back door, so the pain can float away.

Protection from an Ex-partner

Ingredients

1 red candles

Rosehip her

Resin

Lavender oil

Hoodoo Doll

Incense stick

Cast your circle and call the four corners

- Light your charcoal and add the rosehip, lavender and the resin.
- Hold the hoodoo doll above the smoke and chant the following spell: "*I bind you from doing harm to me, yourself and others. Be gone from my life and stop causing me strife. So mote it be*"
- Anoint the candle with the lavender oil (this time from the middle outwards). Think of the person leaving you alone.
- Light the candle and incense and while circling the candle with the incense. Chant the spell 3 times: "*Bring light back to my life so I can clearly see what has been done is now in the past and now I'm free. So mote it be*".
- Take the hoodoo doll and put it in a dark place somewhere safe and do not disturb it until all has settled and is back to normal
- Put the leftover wax at your back door, so the pain can float away.

Be Aware

When working with a Ouija board, always follow these simple rules:
- Be respectful.
- Cast a protective circle.
- Ask positive questions.
- Do not antagonise the spirit.
- Never use a Ouija board whilst under the influence of alcohol.
- Do not converse with negative spirits.
- Always, always close the session with a "goodbye".
- Always close the circle.

Ouija Protection Spell

Ingredients
1 charcoal disc

Cauldron

Hoodoo Doll- Any colour

Lavender essential oil

Mugwort Herb

Sage Herb

- Cast your circle and call upon the four corners.
- Light charcoal disc and place it in your cauldron. Add your herbs and 10 drops of lavender oil to the cauldron.
- Hold your Hoodoo doll above the smoke and say the following chant the following: "*Protect me as I journey forth. Keep me safe as I delve into the spirit spree. Keep me safe three times three. As Spirits of good come to me. Bring to me the news I need. Fill it with positivity. To help me live life three times three. So mote it be*"
- Do this spell before working with a Ouija board and keep the hoodoo doll near whilst working with it.

Spirit Protection Resin - A resin to block out evil

Ingredients
1 charcoal disc

1 Jar

Cauldron

Yellow Jasper or Red Cornelian

Resin

Mugwort Herb

Sage Herb

- Cast your circle and call upon the four corners.
- Light your charcoal disc and place it in the cauldron.
- Add Sage, Mugwort and your resin of choice to the cauldron.
- Empty all your remaining ingredients, including your crystal, into the jar and close the jar.
- Circle the jar around the smoke and chant the following spell:

    "Smoke be, smoke see,

    Resin protect me.

    In my workings, keep me safe,

    Protect me with spirit grace.

    Three times three, let it be.

    So mote it be"

Blessings for the home

Ingredients

Lavender

Rosemary

Sage

Witches Salt or Himalayan salt

- In a pestle and mortar, add up all of the ingredients and grind them together until they become a powder. You can do this in a small quantity for single-use or do it in a larger quantity and transfer the powder to a jar for multiple blessings.
- Walk around the inside of your home (you can also do this outside of your home if you wish) and sprinkle the powder along the doorways and windowsills whilst saying:

    "Smoke of Air,

    And Fire of Earth,

    Cleanse and bless this home and hearth.

    Drive away all harm and fear.

    Only good may enter here.

    So mote it be".

Book of Shadows Blessing Spell

Ingredients
Sage
Mugwort
White Candle
Purple candle
Pentagram

- Call the four corners and light your cauldron.
- Put your white candle and purple candle next your pentagram and Book of Shadows, and then light them.
- Add Sage and Mugwort to the cauldron.
- Place your right hand on your Book and your left hand on the pentagram.
- Then chant the following:

    "Oh, purple and white light, bless this tool be.
    Help my words of wisdom see the visions of me.
    Pentagram I ask of thee,
    To bind my spell and workings be.
    Oh, Book of Shadows hold the key,
    To help and record my workings for me.
    Oh Gods and Goddesses of old,
    Help me make my spell behold;
    The light of love of bless be,
    To work my magic just to see,
    That everything I do comes three by three.
    Bless it be. So mote it be".

Happiness Spell

Ingredients

Cauldron

Orange oil

White Candle

Hoodoo Doll

- Cast your circle and call in the four corners.
- Light your cauldron, and then add 3-4 drops of orange oil into the cauldron.
- Hold your open hands over the smoke and meditate on what happiness you would like to manifest.
- Visualise this thought moving to your hands and then push the thought and the smoke away from you.
- Light your white candle and chant the following spell: *"With this white light I bring only love and light"*.
- Get your Hoodoo Doll and add 3-4 drops of orange oil onto the doll and add 2-3 drops into your cauldron.
- Hold the doll over the smoke whilst thinking of the happiness it will bring you and chant:
    > *"May I be good without any bad.*
    > *May I be happy and never sad.*
    > *I ask of you this very hour,*
    > *Bring this to life with your Divine power. So mote it be."*

Abundance of Joy

Ingredients
3 Green candles

Lavender Oil

Hoodoo doll

Pen and paper

- Anoint your candles with the lavender oil from the centre outwards and place them in a row.
- Take a strip of paper and write the name of the person you want to receive the results of this spell.
- Take a second piece of paper and write something you would like them to receive (for example; love, happiness, health).
- Then take the final piece of paper and write the month that you would like this spell to take effect.
- Light your candles.
- Hold your Hoodoo doll in your non-dominant hand. Then chant the following:

>*"With Mother Earths Blessings- I ask for seeds,*
>
>*To ensure this spell succeeds.*
>
>*I cast my wish into healing fire,*
>
>*To grow the seeds of what I desire,*
>
>*So mote it be".*

- Then set each piece of paper alight with one candle each and place them into your cauldron to burn.
- Let all the candles burn out on their own and wait until the month you chose for the effects of the spell to manifest.

Blessings for your Altar

Ingredients

Altar cloth

3 beeswax candles

Purification tea

Palo Santo wood

- Light your cauldron and light your 3 candles.
- Fold your Altar cloth in half three times. Add the purification tea to your cauldron.
- Light the Palo Santo Wood and smudge it in a clockwise circle over the cauldron.
- Hold the altar cloth over the cauldron. Then chant the following:
    "I bless this be,

    To keep my altar free,

    From negativity three times three.

    By the power of nature's bee,

    This I bless for all to see,

    So mote it be"

Money to Me 3x3

Ingredients
3 green candles
1 Hoodoo Doll
Dragons Spark tea
Bath salts
Lavender Oil

- Light your cauldron and anoint your candles from top to middle then bottom to middle.
- Light the candles and hold your Hoodoo doll in your left hand.
- Add the Dragon's Spark tea to your cauldron.
- Then chant the following:

    "Hoodoo Doll bring me,

    Financial blessings, three times three.

    Bless my life to be debt free.

    Help my path for me to see.

    From Goddess above,

    To Gods below,

    Bring security three times three to my home.

    So mote it be"

- When home, place some Dragon's Spark tea and a few drops of lavender oil to some bath salts and use in the bath- or on your shower base.

Heal a broken heart spell

Ingredients

1 charcoal disc

Cauldron

1 Pink spell candle

Spell candle holder

Goats Rue Herb

Rose Quartz or Tree of Life charm

House of Cleansing or White Sage resin (optional)

- Cast your circle and call in the four corners.
- Light your charcoal disc and place it in your cauldron.
- Add Goats Rue Herb and a resin of your choice to cleanse yourself fully (the resin is optional but boosts cleansing effect).
- Next, place your pink candle in the holder and chant the following before lighting it: *"When I set this wick alight, open my heart to receive healing light"*.
- Then light the spell candle.
- Take your Rose Quartz crystal or Tree of Life charm and visualise a healing pink light surrounding it.
- Then picture a pink cord connecting your heart chakra to the Rose Quartz or charm.
- After you have visualised this, repeat the following:

    "My this cord never let go,

> *I allow it to sew my broken heart closed.*
> *Although I was hurt, I heal from the pain,*
> *And welcome the love I'm bound to gain.*
> *So mote it be"*

- Either keep your Rose Quartz or charm on your Altar or, carry it with you or place it under your pillow.

Money and Good Fortune Spell

Ingredients
1 Charcoal disc

Cauldron

Hoodoo Doll

1 Yellow Spell candle and candle holder

Burdock Herb

Catnip Herb

Citrine Crystal

- Cast your circle and call the four corners.
- Light your charcoal disc and place it in your cauldron.
- Add your Burdock and Catnip Herb to the cauldron. Then, light your spell candle.
- Take your Citrine crystal in your left hand and hold it over the spell candle.
- Repeat the following chant:

    "I bring to me the fortunes of three times three.

    Three times three bring it to me.

    I bless this stone to see for me,

    The blessings I want to see.

    So mote it be"
- Then take your Hoodoo Doll in your right hand, then repeat this chant three times:

> *"Hoodoo Doll a gift to me,*
> *Of good Fortunes for all to see.*
> *So mote it be"*

- Let the candle burn fully and keep the Hoodoo Doll and crystal with you for the spell to take effect.

Ward off Evil spell

Ingredients
1 Charcoal disc and cauldron

Hoodoo Doll

Black candle and candle holder

Salt

Mugwort Herb

Sage Herb

- Before the spell, do any housework that needs to be done.
- Cast your circle and call upon the four corners.
- Light your charcoal disc and place in your cauldron.
- Add your Mugwort to the cauldron and repeat the following:

    "Evil Spirit 1-2-3,

    Stay clear away be gone from me,

    Mighty Hecate banish evil from my sight."

- Then light your black candle and repeat three times:

    "Candle Black, wick of light,

    Banish evil from my sight"

- Add Sage to the cauldron.
- Hold your Hoodoo Doll over the smoke and chant the following:

    "I ask mighty Hecate to come onto this Doll.

    Energies 3x3 bring to thee.

    To ward off evil that is sees.

> *The Doll of protection it shall be.*
> *So mote it be."*

- Always leave the doll facing your front door.
- Sprinkle salt along the front of the door and leave the candle wax at the back of the house.

Bring Back Balance Spell

Ingredients

1 Charcoal disc

Cauldron

Hoodoo Doll

Red spell candle and candle holder

Passionflower Herb

Dandelion Herb

1 Mojo Bag

- Cast your circle and call upon the four corners.
- Light your charcoal disc and place it in your cauldron.
- Add your herbs to the cauldron.
- Then hold your Hoodoo Doll over the smoke and repeat the following 3 times:

    "In this world of unbalanced energy,

    I see a world of trauma that has come upon me.

    Bring in Mother Goddess for all to see,

    To bring back balance I need for me.

    So mote it be."

- Light the red spell candle and place the remaining herbs into a mojo bag.
- Then, hold the mojo bag over the candle and repeat the following 3 times:

> *"Red candle, red candle, bring to me,*
>
> *The balance of life for me to see.*
>
> *So mote it be."*

- Place the Hoodoo Doll and your Mojo bag somewhere in your kitchen to allow the spell to take effect.

Ostara Moonlight Spell

Ingredients
1 Charcoal disc

Cauldron

1 Purple spell candle and candle holder

Mugwort Herb

Resin

Lapis Lazuli Crystal

Cast this spell at night during Ostara. If you can, allow moonlight into the room or casting area.

- Cast your circle and call upon the four corners.
- Light your charcoal disc and add it to your cauldron.
- Add your resin of choice and the Mugwort herb into the Cauldron.
- Light your purple candle and chant the following 3 times:
    "Underneath Ostara's Moon,
    My dreams will sprout, grow and bloom".
- Then, take your Lapis Lazuli crystal and place it in direct moonlight. Visualise whatever desire you have projecting from the crystal to the moon, then say the following:
    "I cast my wish into the moon,
    My heart's desire will reach me soon.

> *Under the moonlight my life starts anew, With Ostara'sik blessing my dreams come true. So mote it be".*

- Leave your Lapis Lazuli to charge in the moonlight overnight and let your spell candle burn down fully.
- Keep your crystal with you for the spell to take effect.

Making your own Spells

In this section you are encourage to make up your own spells.

1. Think of what spell you want to perform.
2. List your ingredients.
3. Instructions on mixing and adding your ingredients.
4. Your spell chant.
5. What to do after.

Remember that spells are supposed to be simple and easy to follow.

Look through the list of items and match them to the spell you want to create.

You may use as many items as you like and then add them to whatever you want to and in any sequence you desire. When you have completed your spell remember to record it in your Book of Shadows.

If you are creating a Mojo bag remember to place it in an appropriate place. The same goes with crystals and hoodoo dolls.

Always ensure that you are in a safe and secure place when you practice magic, where there are no interruptions that may distract you.

You may want to start your own coven which is a group of like-minded people who want to practise magic. Covens often have a head witch so choose wisely those who you wish to be involved with.

Now have a play about and start inventing your own spells.

Spell Work
Name of Spell

Ingredients

Method, or what to do

Chant:

Spell Work
Name of Spell

Ingredients

Method, or what to do

Chant:

Spell Work
Name of Spell

Ingredients

Method, or what to do

Chant:

Spell Work
Name of Spell

Ingredients

Method, or what to do

Chant:

Spell Work
Name of Spell

Ingredients

Method, or what to do

Chant:

Spell Work
Name of Spell

Ingredients

Method, or what to do

Chant:

Spell Work
Name of Spell

Ingredients

Method, or what to do

Chant:

Spell Work
Name of Spell

Ingredients

Method, or what to do

Chant:

Spell Work
Name of Spell

Ingredients

Method, or what to do

Chant:

Spell Work
Name of Spell

Ingredients

Method, or what to do

Chant:

Spell Work
Name of Spell

Ingredients

Method, or what to do

Chant:

**Spell Work
Name of Spell**

Ingredients

Method, or what to do

Chant:

Spell Work
Name of Spell

Ingredients

Method, or what to do

Chant:

Spell Work
Name of Spell

Ingredients

Method, or what to do

Chant:

Spell Work
Name of Spell

Ingredients

Method, or what to do

Chant:

Spell Work
Name of Spell

Ingredients

Method, or what to do

Chant:

Spell Work
Name of Spell

Ingredients

Method, or what to do

Chant:

Spell Work
Name of Spell

Ingredients

Method, or what to do

Chant:

Spell Work
Name of Spell

Ingredients

Method, or what to do

Chant:

Spell Work
Name of Spell

Ingredients

Method, or what to do

Chant:

Conclusion

I hope that you have found this book easy to understand and will find the pathway to Wicca and Spells a pleasant and good experience.

It is important for you to realise that there are no set rules as to what you must do; just remember the basic principles and you can't go wrong.

Good luck and May the Goddess bestow upon you her blessing three times three.

Principles to remember

- The law of three times three.
- Never put out negative spells.
- Learn and understand the tools of your trade.
- Make it simple and easy.
- Don't over-spend on your items.
- Always cast a protective circle.
- Always call in the four corners.
- Record all your experiences and feelings.
- Never force a spell on someone.
- Make time for yourself to learn more.
- Use the internet for anything information you are unsure of.
- Never do a spell when you feel in a bad mood.
- Cleanse and bless your tools before and when you have used them.

"Blessing to you three time three and may your life be filled with joy, peace and happiness. So mote it be"

Printed in Great Britain
by Amazon